GOD WILL
MAKE A WAY

GOD WILL
MAKE A WAY

GWEN CAMPBELL

XULON PRESS

Xulon Press
2301 Lucien Way #415
Maitland, FL 32751
407.339.4217
www.xulonpress.com

Unless otherwise indicated, Scripture quotations taken from the New King James Version (NKJV). Copyright © 1982 by Thomas Nelson, Inc. Used by permission. All rights reserved.

Scripture quotations taken from the Holy Bible, New International Version (NIV). Copyright © 1973, 1978, 1984, 2011 by Biblica, Inc.™. Used by permission. All rights reserved.

Printed in the United States of America.

ISBN-13: 978-1-54566-871-9

1 Corinthians 10:13

"No temptation has overtaken you except that which is common to man; but God is faithful, who will not allow you to be tempted beyond that you are able, but with the temptation will always make the way of escape, that you may be able to bear it."

DEDICATION

T o my wonderful, miraculous, indescribable heavenly Father, who has always been with my girls and me. He has always made a way for us to fulfill His plan and purpose for our lives.

In memory of my deceased father, Allie Keesee, who probably wanted the best for me but didn't know how to show it.

In memory of my deceased mother, Nannie Morton Keesee, who prayed for me and raised me in the nurture and admonition of the Lord, the best she knew how. She was, to me, the **best** mom in the whole world, who loved the Lord with all her heart.

In memory of my spiritual mentor and spirit-filled intercessor, whom God appropriately placed in my life at the right time. Wow! What a blessing she was.

To my two beautiful daughters, Robin and Wendy, with whom the Lord blessed me in the midst of a horrific situation. Thank you, Lord, for bringing us through the valley of the shadow of death.

Finally, to all of you who are experiencing domestic violence or may know someone who is, I dedicate this book to you, so you may know that God will make a way of escape for you too.

A SPECIAL THANKS

A special thank you to my friend Mary Royster, who spent countless hours editing my book to help me get it into a printable format.

CONTENTS

AUTHOR'S PREFACE

G od Will Make a Way: A friend of mine asked me to write about my testimony for a chapter of her book. I agreed to do so and wrote the chapter. After asking my pastor to read what I had written, she said, "You have got to get this in print, because it's going to bless so many who read it."

I live in Durham, North Carolina, and after working with the Durham Crisis Response Center Crisis Line for a year, I decided my pastor was right. Especially after listening to the cries for help from the women calling the crisis line, I decided that I really did need to make the chapter into a book.

As I researched the National Statistics on Domestic Violence, I was even more convinced of the need to write the book. I viewed their website at https://ncadv.ort/statistics to compile the following information:

On average, nearly twenty people per minute are physically abused by an intimate partner in the United States. During one year, this equates to more than ten million women and men.

One in three women and one in four men have been victims of some form of physical violence by an intimate partner in their lifetime.

One in four women and one in seven men have been victims of severe physical violence by an intimate partner in their lifetime.

On a typical day, there are more than 20,000 phone calls placed to domestic violence hotlines nationwide.

The presence of a gun in a domestic violence situation increases the risk of homicide by 500 percent.

Intimate partner violence accounts for 15 percent of all violent crime. 19 percent of domestic violence involves a weapon. Only 34 percent of people who are injured by intimate partners receive medical care for their injuries.

Domestic victimization is correlated with a higher rate of depression and suicidal behavior.

It is my prayer that through my testimony in this book, the amount of domestic violence in our nation will decrease throughout generations to come.

Apostle Gwen Campbell
Durham, North Carolina

CHAPTER 1

GOD'S PROMISES

This little book is written for anyone who might have a doubt or concern that God will always make a way. God will always make a way for you, regardless of what your situation may be. The story of my life and my testimony should convince you of that truth.

In **John 14:6b**, He promised to make a way. Jesus said to him, "I am the way, the truth, and the life." Jesus said this to Thomas, one of His disciples, but it is meant for all of His disciples today. If He is the way—and He is—surely He can make a way for whatever we need in our lives. My prayer is that God will use this testimony to lift you up out

1

of your place of despair and put you on the path to your God-given destiny.

Before I go on, I need to answer the question that you may find yourself pondering in your mind, and that is, "Why would God move on my behalf in my horrific situation?" First of all, God is no respecter of persons, and He shows no partiality. "Then Peter opened his mouth and said: In truth I perceive that God shows no partiality" (**Acts 10:34**). So what He will do for one, He will do for another. Second, although I lived a life of fear for many years, I believed in God. So you have to believe in God and believe that He wants to help you because He loves you. **Hebrews 11: 6b** says, "He is a rewarder of those who diligently seek Him." To me, this scripture says that when we get in trouble, God will help us if we diligently seek Him, and that is what I did. Third, I didn't understand everything about God during those turbulent times, but I knew there was a God and He was real to me. Finally, through all of my discouragement and questions, I knew that, ultimately, God was my only hope, and that's what I believed and hung on to. He was my lifeline, and He wants to be yours also.

CHAPTER 2

GROWING UP AT HOME

In my growing up years, I was very timid and insecure. My home life didn't help to change me. My mother was a Christian, but my father was an alcoholic and an abuser. There was very little peace in our home; most of the time, it was filled with chaos.

We lived on a tobacco farm, so we worked really hard in the summertime to get the crops in. In the winter months, we had a break, and that's when my father would drink the most. Every time he came home intoxicated, he would argue with my mother and sometimes beat her. Consequently, I was a nervous and depressed child. Being depressed caused me to cry a lot, and I would sometimes ask God why I had been born. I felt I had no reason for living.

There were nine children in my family; I was the youngest—the baby of the family. Our ages varied quite a bit. By the time I was six years old, seven of my brothers and sisters married and left our home. As a result, only my sister and I were at home to help on the farm.

Life was miserable for my sister and me. Our only reprieve was to go to school or go with our mother to church. Even today, I say, "Praise God for my mother and the church of the living God." We couldn't go anywhere else—not to school games, parties, or anywhere simply for fun.

My sister was four years older than me, and she didn't appear to be bothered by our lifestyle as much as I was. But in hindsight, I think she was, yet she just showed her disappointments in a different way. Sometimes she would slip out and go places by herself; this would get her, and my mother, into trouble. My dad would always blame Mama whenever he found out. He would blame my mother for anything that went wrong.

CHAPTER 3

MY SIXTEENTH BIRTHDAY

S oon before my sixteenth birthday, my parents allowed a young man named Samuel James to come to our house to see me. I appeared to be older than I was because I was tall and never played much with other children; I usually stayed inside the house. In spite of my insecurity, I seemed mature for my age. Sam was actually twenty-two years old, but my parents did not know it.

My older sister knew Sam from church, and she introduced him to me. He sang in the same men's group as her husband. Of course, since church was the only place we could go,

I was able to go with my mother to church to hear the group sing. I honestly had never in my young life heard anyone sing like he did. I was a young Christian, and I'm not sure if it was the anointing or just that the man could sing that attracted me to him! He could rock the church, meaning that most of the church would be on their feet, shouting and dancing, and others would be mesmerized. I think I was in the mesmerized category.

Since he went to church and was the lead singer for this wonderful group, I thought he was going to be my hero, the one who would get me out of my "prison" at home. Little did I know what would follow.

I had just turned sixteen years old when he asked my father if we could get married. Imagine that! Of course, my dad said no, and rightfully so. My mom was devastated with the very thought of this happening. Nevertheless, at the young age of sixteen, I dropped out of school and ran off with this man, believing he was going to take me out of my misery. We got married in Baltimore, Maryland.

CHAPTER 4

THE BEGINNING OF THE ABUSE

I never dreamed that the very next day he would turn into a monster. But that's exactly what happened. It was the beginning of the accusations and the physical abuse. We were married on July 3, 1963, and the next month, I found myself pregnant with our first child. Even though I was young and "ignorant," I realized I was not ready to become a mother. I thank God that in spite of my immaturity and ignorance, my daughter, Robin, grew up to be a talented, gifted young lady.

I was saved and baptized at the age of twelve, so I knew the Lord; I cried out to Him daily during our six months in Baltimore. Life was miserable, and I cried constantly. I was so miserable that I decided to ask my dad and mom if I could come back home. All praise to God, they both readily said yes. They even allowed my husband to come with me. At that time, I was about five months pregnant, and we were able to stay with my parents until after Robin was born. Even in this, God was making a way. He knew my ending before my beginning, and He was going to make sure I reached my destiny.

I thank God for the time we were able to stay at my parents' home, because after Robin was born, I had postpartum syndrome. What a blessing my mother was to me during that time. God was continuing to make a way.

Shortly after Robin was born, we moved out of my parents' house and got an apartment in Danville, Virginia. Then the abuse got *really* bad for me and our baby, Robin. Sam denied that Robin was his child, because she looked like me, not him. He was very dark, and she was lighter skinned, as I am.

Five months after Robin was born, I got pregnant again, and at eighteen, I gave birth to our youngest daughter, Wendy. Sam accepted Wendy as his child because her complexion was darker, as his was, and that seemed to be enough for him to accept her, although she did not look like him either.

After Wendy was born, I got a job working at Danville Memorial Hospital in the housekeeping department. I had to go to work to help pay the bills and keep food on the table. Sam worked for Dan River Mills when he wanted to go to work; other days, he would stay home. When he stayed home, he would keep the children, so I wouldn't have to pay a babysitter and we would have more for household expenses. He was fired from his job at Dan River Mills because of all the missed workdays. Later, he got another job working with a railroad company. That job often took him out of town. It was sheer joy for us until he returned, and then the abuse would start again the minute he came home.

Every day Sam was home, I suffered some sort of abuse. He blamed it on jealousy, accusing me of being unfaithful and threatening to kill me. Almost each day during his time home, He would throw me down and choke and strangle me so badly that I thought any moment would be my last breath. But God! Through all of this, God's hand was there, preserving me. I had made many mistakes, but God was making a way, even though I didn't realize it at the time.

I continued to be abused on a daily basis when Sam was home. Our daughter Robin was also continually abused. He continued because he said she wasn't his child. Robin cried a lot, I think because she was afraid of him. Every time he walked in the room, she would start to cry, and that would really make him mad. He would shake her and throw her around. One day when she was six months old, her leg was strangely broken and had to be put in a cast. I could not explain to the doctor how it happened, although I had a good idea. The doctor and I decided she probably got her leg caught in her crib. I knew better, but I was afraid to speak out. I knew he had done it somehow.

The times Sam would stay home from work and keep the children created significant chaos. This was not a good thing to do at all. One day at work, I got a phone call from him, asking me to come home because he wasn't sure if he had killed Robin or not. I was terrified on the way home, but when I got there, praise God, she was still alive! He had thrown her against the wall so hard, feces came out of her little body and stuck to the wall. But God! God had a plan for Robin, and the devil couldn't take her out. When there seemed to be no way out, even then, God was making a way. After that, I didn't leave the girls alone with him anymore.

Through all of my mistakes—being rebellious, running away from home, and marrying a man I had only known for three months, God was still with us. He was making a way of escape for my girls and me, according to **1 Corinthians 10:13**: "No temptation has overtaken you except that which is common to man; but God is faithful, who will not allow you to be tempted beyond what you are able, but with the temptation will always make the way of escape, that you may be able to bear it."

CHAPTER 5

MEETING MY
PRAYER WARRIOR

While working at the hospital, I met a wonderful Spirit-filled Christian woman. I will never forget her as long as I live, and I know one day I will meet her again in heaven. God strategically put this lady in position to meet me, and she became my mentor and my Spirit-filled prayer partner. Once again, through the mistakes and the mess I had made of my life, the favor of God was upon me. He was still with me, preparing a way of escape.

When I first met her, I had no idea of the impact she would have on my life. But God did. It was His setup. He was in the process of making a way of escape for my girls and me. Being the great Spirit-filled prayer warrior she was, she already knew that I was a part of her assignment. Even now, thinking about her brings tears to my eyes. She was a wonderful woman who loved and revered God, and she was full of wisdom as she followed and obeyed His voice. At this point in my life, God knew she was exactly what I needed to make it through, as things continued to get worse.

We both worked in the housekeeping department of the hospital, so we were able to talk and pray together every day at work. We would actually go into our supply closet to pray; we called it our prayer closet. Oh, how I thank God for this woman of prayer!

When I was growing up, most Sundays, we would go to Sunday school and stay for the church service, but that was about the extent of my Christian experience. I knew how to pray and cry out to God for help, but I didn't know how to pray effectively. I didn't know that the effectual, fervent prayers of the righteous avail much, according to **James 5:16b**. Most of my prayers were pitiful prayers crying out for help; I knew God heard me, but I didn't know whether or not He would deliver me out of the mess I had made of my life. I believed it was my fault, and in those days, we were told, "If you make your bed hard, you will have to lie in it." But deep down inside of me, I knew God was my *only* hope. I knew God loved me, because He gave His Son to die for me, but I had no clue of the great love He personally had for *me*. As I said earlier, I knew He must have had a plan for our lives, because He kept making a way of escape for us. When I discovered **Jeremiah 29:11 (NIV)**, I was convinced of that. "'For I know the plans I have for you,' declares the Lord, 'plans to prosper you and not to harm you, plans to give you a hope and a future.'"

So, this mighty prayer warrior, the woman God placed in my life, prayed for me constantly, whether we were at work or not. Sometimes at home, when I would be at my lowest point, feeling like I couldn't go one step further, I could feel her praying for me. This would enable me to make it through another day.

Because of my husband's ability to sing, we would go to church almost every Sunday so he could sing with his men's group. The man would literally rock the church. Almighty God had given him a gift to sing, and it was phenomenal. But after church, often before we would even get home, all hell would break loose. He would yell that some man was looking at me, or anything else he could think of to give him an excuse for the abuse. But praise God for Monday mornings; I would go to work and see my mentor and prayer warrior. I would tell her about the abuse, and her words of wisdom, prayer, and advice would show me how to trust God and get the strength to get through another day. She never actually talked about my husband in a bad, derogatory way, but always about survival for my girls and me.

Day by day, things continued on in the worst way imaginable. The strangulations, the terrifying of Robin...he even shot his gun in the house. In those days, we had an old washing machine that had two rollers to run your clothes through to wring out the water. Sam decided to stick Robin's arm in those rollers. But God! Again, He made a way; I was able to withdraw her arm, and she was okay.

One might ask—and some did ask—"Why don't you do something?" I even asked myself that, but the answer was that I was afraid to do anything. In stronger words, I was terrified! Sam always said that if I left, he was going to kill me, and I believed him because of his past actions. It seemed it was inevitable either way. If I stayed, sooner or later, he would have killed me, and if I left, I would have been taking a chance on being killed.

As I stood at the stove cooking our dinner one evening, he sat in the kitchen with his gun, and he decided to shoot it; the bullet went right pass me and through the kitchen window. He simply said, "I barely missed you." But God! Again, even with my mistakes and my rebellion against my parents, God was *still* keeping me and making a way of escape. But I didn't understand this at the time.

CHAPTER 6

An Open Door

I continued to meet with my spiritual mentor and prayer partner at work. Thank God for this woman! She told me, "You cannot leave until God says so." Those were not the words I wanted to hear, but I trusted her, and moreover, I trusted God in her. So I waited, still continuing being abused. One morning as I was preparing to go to work, for the first time in my life, I clearly heard the voice of God. It was not an audible voice, but in my spirit, I heard Him say, "Today is the day for you to leave." I took the children to the babysitter and went to work. When I got there, I met my spiritual prayer partner coming down the hall. When I reached her, the first words out of her mouth—as you've probably already guessed—were, "Today is the day for you to leave." Wow! God was confirming His word and making a way.

I went straight to my supervisor and asked for the day off, and she said yes. I went home as fast as I could and packed as many clothes as I could for the girls and me. God was making a way of escape! I went to the babysitter's house to pick up the girls, then to my mom's house. I did not want to go there because I knew that would be the first place he would look for me, but I had nowhere else to go.

In hindsight, I know this was all a part of God's provision—no matter what it looked like. I understand why my spiritual mentor said I couldn't leave until God said so. If I had done so earlier, I would not have had His hand of provision and protection. **He knew the perfect time.**

Prior to this time, when my parents came to visit us, they knew things were bad. I didn't talk to them about the abuse, but they could sense it. They didn't visit often; Daddy did not like being around Sam. For that reason, I praise God that my dad was not home when Sam got off work and discovered we were gone. He came straight to my parents' house. Dad's absence was surely part of God's plan. God truly set it all up, making a way.

Sam came up to my parents' front door and knocked. I said, "Please, don't anyone go to the door." My sister was at my mom's house at the time, and I had to really convince her to not go to the door. So Sam began to plead with me to come outside, promising that he didn't have the gun and he wasn't going to hurt me. He said he just wanted to talk to me, but I said, "No, I'm not coming out, because I know you have the gun." His next words were, "If you don't come out, I'm going to kill myself." No one in the house believed he would do it, and I knew his real plan was to kill me. After a while, the talking ended, and we heard a gunshot. Sure enough, he shot himself just above the heart and was taken to the hospital where I worked by the person who brought him to my parent's home.

After Sam knew I wouldn't come out, I believe he felt that he had lost the battle, so he wanted to end it all by taking his own life. It happened on a Friday, and when I went to work on Monday, I went to his room to see him. The 22-caliber bullet was lodged in his back, and the doctors couldn't get it out. They said he would be able to live with it. Some of his friends felt sure I was going to go back to him after this had happened, but my answer was, "No!" I knew God had made a way of escape, and I was not going to mess that up! Never did I ever want to go back to that way of living!

I asked to have a meeting with Sam's doctor and a panel of medical professionals to see if they could have him evaluated to find if there was something mentally wrong with him. It was agreed that he would be sent to a mental hospital in Petersburg, Virginia, to be checked out. They kept him for two weeks, and I got a letter stating that he had been released and they found nothing mentally wrong with him. The letter even stated that he was just a mean person. God had so strategically set up our escape that, after Sam left the hospital, I never saw him again.

CHAPTER 7

LEARNING TO FORGIVE

G od is so faithful, and He had so deeply touched my heart about forgiveness. I must say that forgiveness was not something I knew much about at that time, and I did not know how important it is. I knew I was one who never held grudges against someone, but this was a totally different scenario. Sam was someone who had literally made my life, in my estimation, as close to hell on earth as one could get. So for the second time, I clearly heard the voice of God as He spoke to me in my spirit, saying, "You must forgive him." Honestly, to my surprise, I had no problem doing that whatsoever. I knew then that it had to be God, because there was no way that I could have forgiven Sam myself. I even prayed that the next person he dated or married would not have to go through what I did and that God would somehow change him. But I also knew Sam had to want to be changed, and I prayed that prayer for an extended amount of time.

I continued to live with my parents and work at the hospital. I didn't know where Sam went after he was released from the mental hospital, but I assumed that he probably came back to Danville, so I had to be very careful and watchful in my traveling. One Saturday afternoon, he stopped by my parents' house to see the girls, but I had just walked over to my sister's house and missed him. God was still making a way!

While Sam was at my parents' house, my dad sat on the front porch with his loaded shotgun on his lap. I was told my husband went across the street to the neighborhood store and bought the girls each a candy bar, and that was the last time they saw him. At that point, I felt it best that the girls and I should leave Danville. So in November 1968, we moved to Lynchburg, Virginia, to live with an aunt, my father's sister. I was twenty-one years old, and the girls were three and four.

Sam and I were married for four and a half years, and those were four and a half years of pure torture. But God made a way of escape. Even though I had married this man by choice, through ignorance and rebellion, God still showed His grace, mercy, and great love for my girls and me, because He had another plan. He had a better plan, to give us a future and a hope, as recorded in **Jeremiah 29:11 (NIV)**: "For I know the plans I have for you, declares the Lord, plans to prosper you and not to harm you, plans to give you hope and a future."

CHAPTER 8

THE MOVE TO LYNCHBURG, VIRGINIA

Approximately eight months after arriving in Lynchburg, Virginia, I met my second husband, Elisha E. Campbell, whom we called Sonny. We dated for three and a half years before we were married. He had been married before and also had two children. He was very distinguished and mature, and he was fifteen years older than me. Before we were married, we discussed the age difference at length. It was a real concern for him, but not for me. One of the main things that drew me to him was that he not only loved me, but he loved my girls. We were a package; any man who loved me would have to love them too. So at the age of twenty-four, I entered into my second marriage with a man who was thirty-nine.

Prior to Sonny and I getting married, I needed to divorce my first husband, Sam. I did not know what to do about getting a divorce from him, since I did not know his whereabouts. Several months before my second marriage, Sonny took me to see his lawyer, whom he knew and trusted. The lawyer told me that since I didn't know where Sam was, the procedure, at that time, would be to run the request in the newspaper for a certain amount of time, and if I didn't hear from him during that time, we could proceed with the divorce. And that's what happened. I was a little nervous about doing that, for fear that he might find me, so I was very happy not to have heard from him.

When Sonny and I first met, I basically had nothing—just a small-time job at Virginia Baptist Hospital in the housekeeping department. After all, I had dropped out of high school at the age of sixteen, so I did not have a high school diploma. Sonny encouraged me, saying that I could do better. Consequently, I only worked at the hospital for a little while before getting a job at Craddock and Terry Shoe Corporation in the sample shoe department. This was a step up for me in the work force. I stayed on that job for about a year, and he continued to encourage me that I could still do better than that. So my next job was for General Electric Company in the mobile radio department. The pay and benefits for this job were really good, which enabled my girls and me to get our own apartment and move from my aunt's house.

Sonny worked for Babcock and Wilcox Naval Nuclear Fuel Division as a supervisor. After we were married, he lived in the apartment with us for about six months. We later moved into a house he owned. He was a man who believed in taking care of his family. So needless to say, after all we had gone through, the girls and I felt that we were rich! The only thing I had to do was put gas in the car and drive it. I paid no utility bills, nor anything pertaining to our daily living expenses. Sonny felt that I needed a credit card to build my credit, so he helped me obtain one. He believed everyone needed to have a good credit line. Most of the money I earned went into a savings account and toward buying whatever my girls and I needed. The Lord had blessed me with a man who was a wonderful provider. There was such a contrast between the good and bad parts of my life. I could not thank and praise my God enough!

CHAPTER 9

GOING
BACK TO SCHOOL

As the girls grew older, I decided to go back to school. Sonny encouraged me and willingly helped me accomplish my dream, even doing much of the cooking. I worked during the day and went to school at night to earn my GED. Sonny was gracious enough to allow me to do that by helping out with the girls when they needed it. Praise the Lord! Again, even though I had made many mistakes early in life, God showed me favor and allowed me to redeem the time I had lost. Truly, He was still making a way!

If you are a high school dropout or you know of someone who is, please understand that God will make a way for you to move forward and complete your education. He is a good, good Father, and His desire is to always prosper us and move us forward.

After I received my GED, I enrolled in Central Virginia Community College to continue my education. I took evening classes, so it took me longer to finish the courses in which I was enrolled. I remember some Saturdays I would be in the house all day studying, particularly business math and accounting. I did not like those classes, so I had to really put all I had into them, and it paid off. I was able to receive certificates in bookkeeping and general clerical. It was all worth the long hours I spent studying.

After seventeen and a half years of working at General Electric, I was laid off and later went to work for Grace Lodge Nursing and Assisted Living Facility. While there, I held several positions. My entry-level position was in general clerical work. I moved through several other positions, and by taking medical training through numerous workshops, I was grandfathered into the position of Medical Records Director.

While working there, I went back to school again, taking evening classes at Christian Life School of Theology. The main campus was in Columbus, Georgia, but I attended a local campus in Lynchburg. I earned a Bachelor's degree in Theology. This was all a part of God's plan, as He was preparing me even more for ministry. My pastor wanted me to continue on and get my master's degree, but I was really getting tired, so I decided to stop with the bachelor's degree.

As you can see, I couldn't die in my first marriage, because God's plan and purpose for my life was not complete. It continued to unfold as He continued to open new doors. And this was also true for my girls. We had not finished our race. We find this truth in Paul's words to Timothy in **2 Timothy 4:7**: "I have fought the good fight, I have finished the race, I have kept the faith."

CHAPTER 10

AGLOW INTERNATIONAL MINISTRIES AND THE CALL TO MINISTRY

When I was laid off from my job with General Electric Company in 1987, I was out of work for a period of time before going to work for Grace Lodge Nursing and Assisted Living Facility. During this time, I was introduced to a Christian Organization called Women's Aglow Fellowship, now known as Aglow International. I attended my first meeting in September 1987. After the first meeting, I could not stop going. I discovered something spiritually different and wonderful. God allowed me to be placed in that ministry so His plan could continue to unfold in my life. He is an awesome God, and He was continuing to make a way for His plan and purpose for my life, bringing me to the place He wanted me to be for His glory.

Aglow was the place where I began to learn more about Jesus and grow and grow in Him. In my earlier years, I never read my Bible very much. Usually, I would go to church, and whatever the preacher said, I received. I never bothered to follow along in the Bible or to check out what he preached in the scriptures. It just so happened that Aglow had a book table with some interesting books on it. I purchased some of the books to study them and compare them with the Bible, which caused me to begin to read my Bible. It was a wonderful time in my life, and I was learning so much about the Lord. The more I read, the more I thirsted for more of Him. So in December 1987, after three months of attending Aglow, I received the baptism of the Holy Spirit. *Wow!* What a difference that made in my life! In fact, it changed my whole life.

The women in the ministry were so real and so authentic; I had never seen anyone like them before. Every time I showed up, they gave me hugs and words of inspiration and encouragement. I was definitely not used to being treated that way in a spiritual setting. We didn't do that in the church I attended, but I could tell these women were real and full of love. They did it not only for me, but for everyone who came to the meetings. God knew this was exactly what I needed, because I had never experienced this kind of love before. These women were pulling me out of the shell in which I had been for years, and it was God's way of letting me know that He loved me.

After I had attended for a while, Aglow began to use me in various positions. The first thing they asked me to do was be the hostess chairman. God had already shown me they were going to ask me to do that, so I didn't really have to pray about it. I loved being in that position because I liked serving people. Needless to say, I did not want to leave the position when they asked me about coming to serve on the leadership board as administrative secretary, but I did because I wanted to obey God. God continued to open door after door for me to move forward in different positions in Aglow. The more I learned and moved forward, the more they would use me for various things. They began calling on me to teach the Word and do ministry in other Aglow fellowships. Churches also started calling me to speak at their women's ministries.

Today, I currently serve as State Prayer Coordinator for the State of North Carolina, and I have for the past seven years. This is my thirty-first year of being a part of the ministry of Aglow International.

In 1993, I clearly heard the Lord say, "I want you to teach and preach my Word." But the door did not open for me to receive a license to preach the gospel until the year 2000, at the Greater Brookville Church in Lynchburg, Virginia. I later applied to be ordained in the same church in 2005. Praise the Lord! I successfully completed the requirements, and I received my ordination certificate. God brought me through it. He was still making a way to get me to where He wanted me to be.

CHAPTER 11

SONNY AND THE GIRLS

My girls had a good relationship with Sonny in their growing-up years, especially when you consider raising teenagers. He treated them like any good father would, with rules they had to follow. When they didn't follow the rules, there were justifiable consequences. In those days, we called it "being grounded." He would take them to teen parties in the neighborhood and go back and pick them up. They used to hate for him to come inside to pick them up; they would say it was embarrassing. We still laugh about how he would come in and snap his fingers and say, "It's time to go." He taught them both how to drive because I just didn't have the nerves for it. They both left home with his blessings in

1983, although Robin graduated from high school in 1982. She attended Central Virginia Community College for a while and decided that wasn't for her, so she enlisted in the United States Army, where she served for six years. Wendy graduated from high school in 1983 and headed off for college in the fall of that year. She graduated from St. Paul's College in 1987 with a BA in Business Administration.

Later in life, they each had one daughter. Wendy's daughter was born first, and she named her Capricia. Robin's daughter was born second, and she named her Kayla. (More to come about Kayla's birth later.) Sonny was my granddaughters' Papa, and he loved them dearly and they loved him. He had nicknames for both of them. He called Capricia "Kitten" and Kayla "Peanut." After his passing, they would not allow anyone else to call them by their nicknames. They said only their Papa could do that.

CHAPTER 12

THE BIG CRASH

On January fifth of the year 2008, my husband of thirty-six years passed away. He died of lung cancer. The cancer was diagnosed in February 2006, and he went into remission after much prayer and treatment, which he bravely and courageously went through. He only allowed me to take him to one chemo treatment; after that, he drove himself to all of them and to the radiation treatments that followed. On October 20, 2007, the cancer returned and metastasized to his brain. This time, the doctors tried a few more radiation treatments, but to no avail, because the cancer had spread to other parts of his body. At this point, my husband was tired and ready to give up the fight. He decided he was ready to go be with the Lord, and I knew in my heart of hearts that was exactly what was going to happen.

As a family, we thought we were prepared for what would take place a little over a couple of months later. On the evening of his passing, we gathered and prayed over him, thanking God that he never suffered very much and was not in a lot of pain, and we released him to the Lord. Two hours later, he was in the presence of Jesus. We prepared for the funeral and went through that quite well, by the wonderful grace of God. Shortly afterward, it hit me like a ton of bricks, and I almost fell apart. Knowing I was a woman of God and a minister of the gospel, I tried to stand strong, but I would come home in the afternoon to an empty house and lay on the floor and scream out to the Lord. My heart was broken. But my Father is a good, good Father and the mender of broken hearts. He also knows what it's like to watch a loved One die, but thank God, there was and is a resurrection. So, day by day, month by month, and year by year, things started getting better.

Our children stood by me in the most magnificent and honorable way. My girls continued to stand by me, making sure I was alright. Although they lived in North Carolina, one of them would come up every weekend for the first year to check on me. I am forever grateful to them for their faithfulness. On the eighth anniversary of his death, in January 2016, the Lord gave me total release. He made a way for me to walk out of grief into His joy and newness of life for this particular time of my life by His precious Holy Spirit, who is our comforter. For the first time, I felt in my heart He was saying, "Enough is enough!"

CHAPTER 13

THE CALL TO
APOSTLESHIP AND THE
SECOND ORDINATION

I n 2004, before Sonny died, I was sitting in my living room preparing a sermon for Sunday morning, when I clearly heard the Lord Jesus Christ Himself say to me, "You are an apostle." Now trust me; that is *not* something I would have come up with on my own. When I look back, I can see He had been using me under the apostolic anointing in the Aglow Ministry. He further said, "When you go in to preach Sunday morning, you will be going in as an apostle."

Oftentimes, women preachers are not accepted in all churches, and I happened to have been one of those women. The pastor of a church I was once invited to told me, "You can teach from the podium on the floor, but you can't stand behind the pulpit." I was one who would see a whole family get up and walk out of the church when I stood up to preach. And, sad to say, when it came to women preachers, some women were worse than the men. After I was licensed, we had one lady leave the church. So I surely wasn't about to tell anyone that I was an apostle.

In 2006, the Lord led me to a wonderful church in Lynchburg: Tree of Life Ministries. In 2009, I asked to meet with the pastor, and I told him that Jesus had told me I was an apostle. He asked me some questions and, basically, said that if Jesus had told me that, then he would certainly accept it. This church was a part of a large denomination known all over the world as the International Pentecostal Holiness Church (IPHC), and he suggested that I become ordained under their denomination. Since I was already ordained, the process did not require as much as it would have for someone who had never been ordained before. I had to read two books and take tests after completing the reading.

Before the exams, I had to meet with the council, or board, of the denomination in our district, and I was readily accepted as a candidate for ordination. They laid their hands on me and prayed over me at the time of the first meeting. After I passed the tests, I had to meet with the council again before the time of ordination. I was asked a series of questions, but in an atmosphere that was comfortable as a time of preparation for ordination. Since it is a huge denomination, my ordination certificate would be recognized all over the world.

This ordination took place on June 18, 2011, just after I moved to Durham, North Carolina, to be near my children. It was even more wonderful than the first one. The ordination was a time of celebration. It was a time of laying on of hands and words of prophesy and affirmation. The one thing they never did was recognize your gift of ministry. They ordained you and said it was up to you to walk in the ministry gift to which you were called. But I knew that more needed to be done to be recognized as an apostle. I already knew I am one because Jesus had said so, but I also knew that there was a commissioning that needed to take place. I was a happy camper being ordained under this ministry, and it felt authentic and ordained of God. So I knew, at some point, the commissioning would come, and I was okay with that.

My cousin, who was a pastor, was also ordained with me on the same day, under the same denomination. She also had been called to be an apostle. As a result, she too knew she needed to be commissioned. Apostles are sent ones, commissioned by the Lord Jesus Christ to go and do the work of an apostle. There are several scriptures that make reference to this, including **Mark 3:14**: "Then He appointed twelve, that they might be with Him and that He might **send** them out to preach, and to have power to heal sicknesses and to cast out demons."

Apostles have to be called to the ministry of apostleship by the Lord Jesus Christ. **Ephesians 4:11-12** says, "And He Himself (Jesus) gave some to be apostles, some prophets, some evangelists, and some pastors and teachers; for the equipping of the saints for the work of ministry, for the edifying of the body of Christ." Some would argue that Jesus stopped with twelve apostles, but these verses clearly shows that it goes beyond the twelve appointed apostles in the four gospels.

Although Jesus commissions and sends spiritually, after the calling of Jesus, we are licensed and ordained ministers by man. We also have to be commissioned by man, and it has to be done by another apostle. So, on March 25, 2012, my cousin and I were commissioned by Apostle Louis Dickens with Victory through Christ International Ministries.

CHAPTER 14

THE MOVE TO DURHAM, NORTH CAROLINA

After being in Durham for about two weeks, I was asked to be the North Carolina State Prayer Coordinator for Aglow International Ministries, and I accepted. Later, I joined Living Waters Community Church, a part of the International Pentecostal Holiness Church denomination. This was the same denomination I was in while in Virginia. I stayed there approximately three years before the Lord connected me with Apostle Shirley R. Brown, Pastor of Destiny International Ministries, SRB Ministries, and No Nonsense Kingdom Alliance (NNKA). About six months before leaving LWCC, I was led to join NNKA. Apostle Brown and I had communicated off and on for a few months, and I found her to be very approachable, very accessible, and willing to help in any way she could. I had never met a pastor quite like her. As an apostle, I knew I needed to be in a place under apostolic leadership and the apostolic anointing. I loved the name "No *Nonsense* Kingdom Alliance," and I knew it was right for me, especially after some of the things I had experienced in my church history, such as my rejection as a woman minister. I want to be clear that none of this is in reference to LWCC. I loved the pastor, his wife, and the members of that great church. They were very good to me, and still are. My leaving had nothing to do with them; I was only obeying the voice of God.

Approximately six months after I became affiliated with NNKA and came under covenant relationship with Apostle Brown, I was led to become a part of Destiny International Ministries. What a joy and blessing this move has been in my life. After having lived in Lynchburg for forty-three years, it was hard leaving. But I realized that I was not sent to Durham just to be near my children; this was all a part of God's plan down through the years to get me to the place where I needed to be—to fulfill His plan for my life and step into my destiny.

While under Apostle Brown's leadership at Destiny International Ministries, I published my first book at the close of 2015, titled, *Unity: God's Perfect Plan for Joyful Living*. God put this book in my heart several years prior to writing it by showing me that it was His heart for His people to live in unity, just as He and His Son do, as described in **John 17: 21**: "That they all may be one, as You, Father, are in Me, and I in You; that they also may be one in Us, that the world may believe that You sent Me." It is a small, quick-read book that covers almost every aspect of life regarding unity. It includes topics about family, churches, team members, and co-workers. Apostle Brown encouraged me to get it done. She seemed more excited than I was because she loves to see people, particularly those under her leadership, fulfill their accomplishments for the Lord. Consequently, God made a way, and another one of His plans unfolded in my life.

CHAPTER 15

SHEKINAH GLORY APOSTOLIC MINISTRY

I n June 2012, God put a ministry in my heart. He gave me the name, vision, and mission statement. The name is Shekinah Glory Apostolic Ministry. The purpose of the ministry is to lead people to Christ and, for those who know Him, into a deeper relationship with Hm. It is also to help people know who they are in Christ and who Christ is in them. The mission statement is as follows:

As an apostle of Jesus Christ and of Shekinah Glory Apostolic Ministry, it is my desire to produce an atmosphere of worship in which God may manifest His presence and His

Glory so that the Shekinah Glory of God can fill the Temple; whether it is in a church setting, market place, or one-on-one ministry. It is to see sinners come to Christ, and the captives set free and restored to walk in their identity to fulfill their destiny. This will be accomplished through teaching, preaching, interceding, exhorting and mentoring. God has anointed me to help people know who they are in Christ, and who Christ is in them, to bring about restoration and empowerment to people to be all God would have them be.

I applied for my EIN number, received it, and tried to get the ministry going, but nothing happened. So I tucked the information for the ministry away in a drawer and left it there until God's timing. I knew better than to try to open a door myself without God's timing or approval.

Through Shekinah Glory Apostolic Ministry, it is my goal to reach the next generation and the "unchurched" for Christ, and to encourage the Body of Christ to be one in the spirit of unity. But still, I had knocked on a few doors that weren't open to me, and consequently, I knew I had to wait on God; His timing is perfect.

A few years later, during one of my conversations with Apostle Brown, she asked me the name of my ministry, and

I said, "I don't have a ministry." As soon as I said it, God brought it to my remembrance by saying, "Yes, you do." So, I explained to her what had happened and told her the name of the ministry, "Shekinah Glory Apostolic Ministry." I retrieved the materials from the drawer, and after reviewing them with her, she persuaded me that it was time to launch the ministry. So, in March 2016, the ministry began. She was excited, and today, Shekinah Glory Apostolic Ministry is up and running for the Glory of God!

As a word of encouragement for those of you who may have dreams and visions that have not yet come to pass, please **do not** give up on them. Sometimes it's just a matter of being positioned correctly, in the right place at the right time. If you know whatever God has put in your heart is from Him, hold on to it, because at the right time, He shall bring it to pass.

Even before my children, my grandchildren, and myself were formed in our mothers' wombs, God had a plan for us. **Psalm 139: 13-16** says,

For You formed my inward parts; You covered me in my mother's womb. I will praise You,

for I am fearfully and wonderfully made; marvelous
are Your works, and that my soul
knows very well. My frame was not hidden from You,
when I was made in secret, and
skillfully wrought in the lowest parts of the earth.
Your eyes saw my substance, being yet
unformed. And in Your book they all were written,
the days fashioned for me, when as
yet there were none of them.

He knew us before we were created, and He knew the things we would encounter in life and how the enemy would try to take us out before His plans were fulfilled. But His answer to the enemy was already, "No," even when I made a serious mistake and ran away to marry my first husband. God knew what was going to happen, and He had already planned the way of escape. He is an awesome God, and nothing catches Him by surprise. He had seen our end before our beginning, before we were born. Hallelujah, and glory to the Lamb of God! I was blessed with a praying mother, and my children had a praying grandmother, and the legacy continues on as I pray for them. **Every** plan God has for us **will** come to fruition.

CHAPTER 16

THE NUMBER SEVEN

Since my move to North Carolina, there has been something about the number seven. The house God told me to buy has the number seven included in its address. I knew this would be the place where I would begin to see all of God's promises being fulfilled. This would be the place of the beginning of the completion of the promises on my life. Notice carefully the two words "beginning" and "completion." As I previously mentioned, after the death of my husband of thirty-six years—at the end of the seventh year, going into the eight year—the Lord released me from the grief of my husband's death and said, "Now step into your new beginning." There have been a number of new beginnings in my life since then.

On June 15, 2017, I turned seventy years old, which means I was born in 1947. The Lord said that in my seventieth year, I was going to really start seeing His plans and promises unfold in my life. And I know this to be true, because He is not a man that He should lie. Greater things are on the horizon for my family and me.

So may I remind you once again that we, as a family, could not die in the rebellious mess I made of my life at the age of sixteen, nor all the other messes in which we found ourselves from time to time. God had a plan for us for His purpose. His awesome grace and mercy cover us as His plan continues to unfold in our lives to get us to His expected end.

CHAPTER 17

UNFULFILLED DREAMS AND VISIONS

As you are reading this book about my testimony, perhaps you may be thinking of people you know who died without fulfilling their dreams and destinies. Please understand, I do know that is too often the case. I've always heard that the graveyard is full of dreams and destines unfulfilled. I cannot tell you that I know all the answers to the reasons why they were not fulfilled, but I do know that we live in a fallen world. It happened when Satan became the god of this world through Adam surrendering his rights to him, as recorded in Genesis, the first book of the Bible. When that happened, sin entered into the world, and we've been in a battle ever since. The good part about the battle is that Jesus has already won it for us. God has always given us free choices, and life is about the decisions we make in and for our lives. The truth is, I made some very bad decisions and choices, but I believed in God and knew He was the only One who could help me.

When it comes to the things of God, I think the key words are "to have faith" and "believe." **Hebrews 11:6** says, "But without **faith** it is impossible to please Him, for he who comes to God must **believe** that He is, and that He is a rewarder of those who diligently seek Him." I can't say that I was a person of great faith in my time of distress, but I did believe. The other key, which is pretty big, is to have someone praying for you. This is **very important**. If at all possible, you should have an intercessor, someone who prays diligently for you. **James 5: 16b** says, "The effective fervent prayer of a righteous man avails much." We become righteous through Jesus Christ by accepting Him as our Savior. When we do that, and pray to the Father in His name, God hears us and will answer our prayers. Remember, my Spirit-filled prayer partner, who worked with me, prayed for me effectively and fervently, and God answered her prayers for me. Also, I *know* my Christian mother prayed for me as well. If you don't have a prayer partner or an intercessor who will commit to pray for you, ask God to give you one, and I believe He will. You must believe that God will help you and meet your needs, because He loves you. **John 3:16** says, "For God so loved the world that He gave His only begotten Son, that whoever believes in Him should not perish but have everlasting life."

God does not want any of us to perish. That's why He sent His Son to save us. He didn't only save us so we could go to Heaven, but He died to also save us from some of the awful things that can happen to us in this life, just like He did for my girls and me. **John 10:10** says, "The thief does not come except to steal, and to kill, and to destroy. I have come that they may have life, and that they may have it more abundantly." So it's Satan, who is known as the thief, who comes to steal and kill, until he totally destroys us, if we allow him to. This is why we need to pray and have others praying with and for us. But Jesus came that we may have an abundant life; He desires for us to have nothing missing and nothing broken in our lives. We must believe those words are true. We must believe the word of God for our lives, because He loves us and cares about us. He is a good, good Father who loves His children.

Again, I say to you that I cannot tell you I have all the answers, but God does. And we have to trust Him with that. But if those we love do die before reaching their destiny on this earth, and if they have accepted the Lord Jesus as their Savior, they will enter the greatest destiny one can imagine, and that is life eternal with Jesus.

So I close this chapter by saying that, for my girls and me, I still believe that the best is yet to come, and we *will* finish, and we *will* finish strong, **because God made a way!**

CHAPTER 18

ADDITIONAL TESTIMONIES OF GOD'S MIRACULOUS POWER

B efore I close this book, I want to share some more testimonies of God's miraculous power in the lives of my family. Hopefully, these testimonies will increase your faith all the more.

My girls inherited beautiful singing voices from their natural father. I could sing a little bit, but that was about it. I knew nothing about music, but I did know when singing sounded good and sounded right. Even though I did not know one note from another, I began to teach them to sing and blend their voices together to make a beautiful sound. Robin is an alto, and Wendy is a strong soprano; this worked out really well when they sang together. They were around four and five when I started teaching them to harmonize. They were only fourteen months apart in age, and they really loved to sing. They took voice and piano lessons and, consequently, learned music quite well. They sang on both the school and church choirs.

Little did I know that God had already ordained Wendy to be a worship leader. The first time I saw her lead worship, I was in awe at the way she could lead the people into the presence of the Lord. I still truly believe that we couldn't die in that first horrible situation we were in because, through much prayer, God had already ordained that His plan was going to go forth in our lives. So I want to remind each of you reading this chapter that God has an ordained plan for your life, and it is my prayer that it will come to pass.

The girls continued to use their voices for the Lord. They have been invited to many places to sing His praises. Robin even worked on a recording, which has not been completed and released as of yet, but that's not the end of the story! She became a licensed minister in 2009 and preaches the gospel of Jesus Christ. Robin has also been called into the ministry of a prophet, and she often operates in that gift. But that's not the end of that story. What God has spoken, we believe shall come to pass in His timing. As mentioned earlier, Wendy and Robin have two beautiful daughters, one each. Kayla is Robin's daughter, and Capricia is Wendy's daughter. They too can sing beautifully, but they are not using their voices yet.

Before Kayla was born, Robin had to have two surgeries because of fibroid cysts on her ovaries. After the second surgery, she had only one ovary and one fallopian tube, and they were opposite each other. Consequently, the doctor informed her that she would never be able to have children, which was scientifically true. But Kayla was born on April 7, 1998. When God says yes, it doesn't matter what the doctor has said. As Kayla was being born, I was there in the delivery room and heard the nurse say, "We still don't know how you are having this baby!" But of course we knew—God had ordained it before she was ever formed in her mother's womb. **Psalm 139:15a** says, "My frame was not hidden from You, when I was made in secret." **Psalm 139: 16a** says, "Your eyes saw my substance, being yet unformed. And in Your book they all were written, the days fashioned for me." We call

Kayla our miracle baby, and God has a special calling for her life into which she has not yet stepped. The enemy has been trying hard to defeat her, but he is a liar; we are praying that she will one day step into her destiny. We are also praying the same for Capricia, because the enemy is trying to blind her into not knowing who she is in Christ. But again, the enemy is a liar, and it is our desire to live by the Word and promises of God. **Joshua 24:15b** says, "But as for me and my house, we will serve the Lord."

After becoming a part of Aglow International Ministries and learning more about the Word of God, I began to learn more about the importance of tithing and sowing seed. **Genesis 8:22** says, "While the earth remains, seedtime and harvest, cold and heat, winter and summer, and day and night shall not cease." This scripture says to me that if you sow seed, you will reap a harvest in some form. It may not be money; although it may be. But it could also be joy, love, peace, health, and so much more.

The following is an example of tithing and sowing seeds. When Kayla was about to enter her sophomore year in college, she needed two summer classes. When she went to register for the classes, she was told in the registrar's office that the funds were not there for those classes, even though Kayla had already been informed that the funds were. Nevertheless, Kayla was told that she had to pay $2,050 to enroll. The night before this happened, I sowed a seed at church. It wasn't a large seed, but it was all I had at the time. It wasn't even the amount the speaker had asked for. But out of obedience, I sowed what I had, and the very next day, the harvest came. Kayla persevered in trying to prove to admissions that the money was there. Finally, through her persistence and the sown seed, they found that the money really had been paid, and all that Kayla owed was $50! All praise to God! He had made a way for the office to find Kayla's money for her summer classes.

On June 27, 2018, I had to have a total knee replacement. The healing process had complications and was taking longer than expected. As a result, I was not able to return to work at the time I had thought. Meanwhile, I knew this young girl who had given birth to a handsome little boy, about four months old, and she had a problem that caused her to need some money. I felt the Lord say, "Sow a seed in her life," and I did. I was obedient and didn't give it any more thought, until I was told the following week that I did not have enough sick leave to cover the extra time I needed to be out of work. The person in Human Relations said my pay would be short for the month of August, and I would also lose my opportunity to stay on the year-round payroll plan. I could not believe what I was hearing. That meant less pay for August and two months without pay next summer. She said my only other choice would be to ask some of the other employees if they would donate me some of their days. I needed fifteen more days to stay current in my pay status. I am one who hates to ask someone for anything, but I had to swallow my pride, which God hates, and ask three other employees I knew for five days of their time. By the grace and goodness of God, and the goodness of their hearts, they all said yes. I immediately remembered the seed I had sown a few days prior to this situation. Once again, God had made a way!

God also delivered my youngest daughter, Wendy, out of a very abusive marriage, similar to mine. But God! She is still here today, glorifying God through song.

As I stated, Robin had female complications with her health for many years, and as a result, she had to have several surgeries. Shortly after I moved to North Carolina, she had to have another surgery. The doctor had found a mass on the one ovary she had left, and the ovary needed to be removed. The doctor told Robin that without ovaries, she would have to go on hormone therapy immediately, but she was believing for a miracle. She had heard about the danger of hormone medication, and she did not want to take it. In fact, she had decided she was not going to take it. She told the doctor, "If you go in and find nothing wrong with my ovary, will you promise me you will not take it out?" The doctor said, "Of course I won't." As it turned out, the ovary did have to be removed. But when the surgery was over and the doctor came out to talk to us, she said in the area where there was no ovary, there was now a perfect ovary in that spot. Nobody but God could do that! How great is our God? Robin left the hospital with a brand-new ovary and no hormone medication.

God also allowed her to purchase a house with basically zero credit. It was prophesied, and God did it!

Robin's most recent miracle was that she had been diagnosed with chronic pancreatitis for several years. A few weeks ago, she got results from a test that was done, and when she visited her doctor for the results, the doctor informed her that the diagnosis could no longer be found.

These are some of the miracles God continued to work in our lives. I can't explain why God does everything He does, but I do know He is a miracle-working God. Maybe some of these things happened due to what we had gone through earlier in our lives. The Bible says in **Proverbs 6:31**, "Yet when he (satan) is found out, he must restore sevenfold." That is seven times of everything he has stolen from us, according to the word of God. If we want it, we have to believe it and expect it. **2 Corinthians 5:7** says, "For we walk by faith, not by sight." This means that we don't live by what we see happening now, but we live by faith in what God said in His Word. **Matthew 24:35** says, "Heaven and earth will pass away, but My words will by no means pass away." This means God watches over His words to perform them.

God has been making a way for everything that He has ordained for us to line up with his plan. As always, He will bring His plans to pass. He has made miraculous ways for His plans to go forth. He is an awesome God, and I believe He will always make a way for you and for me, in one way or another.

ABOUT THE AUTHOR

G wen Campbell is a licensed and ordained minister of the gospel, called to be an Apostle of Jesus Christ. She received her Minister's license in the year 2000, earning a Bachelor of Theology degree in 2005 from Christian Life School of Theology. She was ordained in 2005 and commissioned to be an Apostle in 2012.

Gwen's husband of thirty-six years, Elisha E. Campbell (Sonny) passed away on January 5, 2008. Three years after his passing, after living in Lynchburg, Virginia, for forty-three years, Gwen moved to Durham, North Carolina, where she serves as State Prayer Coordinator for Aglow International Ministries. Gwen has been a part of Aglow for thirty-one years, serving in various roles of leadership for most of those years. Gwen accredits a great deal of her spiritual growth to the Aglow Ministry, for it is the vehicle God used to mature her and prepare her to step into her purpose.

In 2012, the Lord gave her the name "Shekinah Glory Apostolic Ministry" as the ministry she operates under when she's not serving in Aglow. God gave her this name because He desires to see His Shekinah Glory show up in every spiritual meeting. "The Glory of the LORD filled the Temple" **(Ezek. 43:5)**.

She serves as a mentor to many women and has for several years. To see other women reach their potential in the Lord is a passion the Lord gave her.

Gwen attends Destiny International Apostolic Learning Center in Raleigh, North Carolina. In June 2014, God led her to come into covenant affiliation with No Nonsense Apostolic Alliance in Raleigh, under the Leadership of Dr. Shirley R. Brown. In January 2015, she became a part of Destiny, where Dr./Apostle Shirley R. Brown is the Pastor. The ministry is moving her further along into the purpose to which God has called her.

She loves teaching and preaching the gospel of Jesus Christ. Her passion is to see every person step into their true identity to fulfill the purpose to which they were called.

Gwen works for Durham Public Schools as an Instructional Assistant for Exceptional Children. She considers this job to be very rewarding, as this too is a type of ministry.

This is the second book she has written. Her first book was ***Unity: God's Perfect Plan for Joyful Living***. This book was published in the fall of 2015.

It is her desire to give this book to many abused women who have or are suffering from domestic violence, to give them hope and to let them know that God Will Make a Way for them to be free from domestic violence. This book will also be a blessing to others to see the miraculous power of God at work.

To contact Gwen, email her at gwenkc7@gmail.com, or call her at 434-845-7532 (H) or 434-546-2472 (C).

CPSIA information can be obtained
at www.ICGtesting.com
Printed in the USA
FSHW021858260619
59469FS